## Applauding *Laugh Lead Learn Live Lovingly*

I attest to Harriet West Gordon's commitment to "living life lovingly". My relationship with Mrs. Gordon developed through "A David Dance Company" where students of all ages were taught various art forms of dance while building character. She became a surrogate studio-mom, advocate and intercessor for our students and company. I later learned of her personal love of liturgical dance and had the opportunity to watch her minister on numerous occasions with vibrancy and passion. She embodies the purpose of movement both physically and spiritually. Mrs. Gordon is dedicated to exercising her "Faith through examples of her "Works." I am grateful that she is transferring her knowledge and passion which will help others.

**Ladisa Robinson Onyiliogwu**
**Co-founder, Entrepreneur**
**"The GoodLIFE" Company**

Our bodies are not our own; we were bought with a price. So we must be faithful stewards of God's property.
**Madonna Woolford**

**M.S.N., R.N., B.S.N**.

We need to be proactive in health: Mind, Body, Spirit, and Soul.
**Debra Griffin Stevens**

**D.N.P., M.S.N., R.N.C-M.N.N.**

I was taught that love is a powerful weapon with which we have been equipped. In the hands of an irresponsible soldier, it is only a threat. But for committed warriors, it is a powerful force! In her book, Harriet West Gordon gives practical tips on how to incorporate love into our daily lives. I remember at a young age, my mother taught me that prayer is simply communication with our heavenly Father. This is where I experience the full power of love. The insightful tools she offers in this book are full of wisdom and are guaranteed to be life changing.

**Dawn Gordon Smith**

**Wife, Parent, Trainer, M.Ed Educator, Entrepreneur**


We are all works in progress committed to excellence as we grow.

**1K Phew (Glenn "Isaac" Gordon, II)**

**Professional Hip-Hop Artist**


In life we go from one anxious moment to another. We must stop justifying unhappy and unhealthy living habits, then searching for quick fixes to become healthy. This book will assist you with changing your habits, today.

**Glenn D. Gordon**

**Fitness and Sports Enthusiast/B.S. Sociology**

# HARRIET WEST GORDON

# PEEL

## LAUGH LEAD LEARN and LIVE LOVINGLY

NO BRANCH CAN BEAR FRUIT BY ITSELF;

IT MUST REMAIN ON THE VINE.

JOHN 15:4B

# DISCLAIMER

*The information presented herein is in no way intended as a substitute for medical counseling. This book was written to provide experiential information. Neither Harriet, Glenn D. Gordon, GHD Inc., nor any member of the organization's board shall have liability or responsibility to any person with respect to damage, injury, or any alleged causes resulting from information in this book.*

All scripture quotations, unless otherwise indicated, are from the King James Version of the Holy Bible.

Copyright December 2017 by Harriet West Gordon
All rights reserved
No part of this book may be reproduced or retransmitted in any form or by any means without the written permission of the author.

Cover designed by Harriet Gordon
ISBN: 978-0-9862166-4-0

# GOD'S DIVINE HANDWORK, INC.

Our organization's goal is to affect the lives of people in the communities. God's Divine Handiwork, Inc. (GHDI), is a family-oriented organization which has deep concern for the well-being of our society. We desire to see people "well" in all aspects of their lives. We aim to educate society regarding academic, relational, economical, spiritual, emotional, and physical health. Conferences, forums, seminars, classes, and workshops may be arranged for specific needs. Our services include courses titled, but not limited to:

Healthy Living 503
Test-Taking Tips
Time Management
Parenting to the End
PEEL, daily 365 Days of Inspiration
PEEL, Volume 1: Pray Powerfully
PEEL, Volume 2: Eat Efficiently
PEEL, Volume 3: Exercise Enthusiastically
PEEL, Volume 4: Laugh Lead Learn Live Lovingly

Contacts us: **harrietwestgordon.com**
**peelv5@gmail.com** and on Facebook:
**http://www.facebook.com/peelv5**

HarrietWestGordon.com

> "It's the **quality** of your days rather than the **quantity** of your years that really counts.
>
> Enjoy life! "
>
> —Harriet Gordon, LPC

# DEDICATION

---

**Dedicated to my husband, Glenn D. Gordon.** Through the years, we have had to *Laugh, Lead, Learn and Live Lovingly* through it all.
**I love you.**

**PEEL,** Volume 4: *Laugh Lead Learn and Live Lovingly* is dedicated to the Body of Christ who can live victoriously in every area of life – which includes taking care of your ***total*** health and fitness.

# CONTENTS

PREFACE . . . . . . . . . . . . . . . . . . . . . . . . 10

CHAPTER 1 . . . . . . . . . .Laugh . . . . . . . 13

Create an Atmosphere of Joy

CHAPTER 2 . . . . . . . . Lead  . . . . . . . 24

Positioned for Leadership

CHAPTER 3 . . . . . . . . Learn . . . . . . . 39

Charge Your Atmosphere

CHAPTER 4 . . . . . . . . Live . . . . . . . . . 64

Take Care of You, Totally - Evangelism

CHAPTER 5 . . . . . . . Love . . . . . . .  90

The Ultimate Expression

CHAPTER 6 . . . . . . . . Conclusion . . . 100

PEEL ABC's

REFERENCES . . . . . . . . . . . . . . . . . . . 111

ABOUT THE AUTHOR . . . . . . . . . . 112

# ACKNOWLEDGEMENTS

Thank you for your wealth of experience through the years, families:

## West, Gordon, Dunn, Bentley, and Moore

*Special Recognition*
Betty L. Strickland, Ed.D.
Marcia L. Tate – lecturemgt.com
Lakisha Louissaint – Iamlakisha.com
Carla Fields – CarlaFields.com

***My husband, Glenn; daughter, Dawn*** *and family;* ***son, Isaac*** *and family*

# PREFACE

*H*ow many time has your heart been wounded because you expected the people you love to be perfect and perfection eluded them as well? How many times have you beat yourself up for not being perfect? What's so wrong with wanting a happy ending? The answer . . . nothing! That is the whole reason Jesus came, to provide the happy ending for which we all long from deep within us. Can you see it? Boy (Jesus) seeks out "the girl of his dreams" (the Bride of Christ); pursues her; fights for her; rescues her; provides for her; protects her; and, makes it possible for them to live happily ever after for eternity. As He does all of this, she loves him with all of her heart, co-laboring with him for his Kingdom to reign. It is an eternal desire that resides in each of us for a reason . . . because it resides in the heart of our Heavenly Father. It is a choice to come into agreement with the truth of His love for us, how He sees us, and to reject the self-hatred, condemnation and judgment we are so quick to agree with towards ourselves.

Coming into agreement with the truth is a choice to extend this same unconditional love we have received to those around us.  That is grace.  Grace being "unmerited favor".  Though it may sound as if God is only putting up with us.  A more literal translation of grace is – out of God's delight in each of us, He chooses to extend favor rather than to take offense at our sins.  This is real love.  God knows everything about us, more than we know ourselves, and still His desire is to extend His favor to us out of His delight in us.  This gives us more reasons to desire to please God.

Community leaders, pastors, families, and individuals who desire to empower others and themselves will be blessed by this book.  It is impossible to exude healthy nurturing if you are unhealthy.  Proper healthcare can break strongholds in geographical regions and individual lives.  This book serves as a guide on this journey with numerous tips; for example:

*Sunshine* – 15 minutes in the sun will lower your blood pressure.  It also turns your body's cholesterol into Vitamin D.  It is free, use it!

*Water* – Drink lots of it. It will cleanse your body tissues and give you energy.

*When to Eat* – Eat your largest meal in the morning, a moderate lunch, and sparingly in the evenings. Meals should be spaced 4 to 5 hours apart.

*When to Drink* – Drink 15 to 20 minutes before meals or two hours after meals. Drink at least 8 glasses of water per day.
*When to Sleep* – Our bodies heal themselves between 9 p.m. and 12 midnight.

This is the fourth in a series. <u>PEEL Laugh Lead Learn and Live Lovingly Volume 4</u> was prepared with you in mind. Although you are encouraged to read it thoroughly, the chapters have been designed for independent use.

For victory in every area of your life, consider the researched advice from each volume of P.E.E.L.

P.   PRAY POWERFULLY – Vol. 1
E.   EAT EFFICIENTLY – Vol. 2
E.   EXERCISE ENTHUSIASTICALLY – Vol. 3
L.   LAUGH LEAD LEARN LIVE LOVINGLY – Vol. 4

# CHAPTER 1
# LAUGH
## Create an Atmosphere of Joy

"Take life seriously but not yourself; Learn to LAUGH."
Laughter is good medicine.

Can God manifest His laughter on the inside of us where He is literally laughing through us? We have emotions such as, love, joy, and sadness. Within our emotional structure is the ability to laugh. God made us in His image and likeness; therefore, we know that many of our emotions are the same range as the emotions of God.

John 14: 21-23 tells us, "He who has my commandments and keeps them, it is he who loves me. And he who loves me will be loved by my Father, and I will love him and manifest myself to him . . . and we will come to him and make our home with him."

The words, "manifest myself" are literal interpretations. This verse tells us that manifestations from God are possible to receive. If God can manifest some of His emotions on the inside of us where we can actually feel it, then it is only logical to derive that God can also manifest His laughter on the inside of us. God has plenty of joy and happiness within His personality.

As a youth, I can remember bubbling over with laughter – what seemed to me – at the most inappropriate times. For example, my mother often separated her youth during church services for seating assignments.

I recall a specific memorial service. While the widow woman of the deceased, youth, and other family members looked on, a woman stood to speak about the deceased man. She continued to discuss incessantly of how the four of them: the deceased, his wife, the speaker's husband, and the speaker were inseparable. At the end of her remarks, we realized she was speaking admiringly of the first wife of the deceased, as his widow grieved and listened. That was my first experience of an oration of that kind. As a surprised youth, my "tickle box turned over." I was so amused and the laughter would not stop – during a memorial service!

High School added a plethora of opportunities for merriment and laughter, in and around the instructional classrooms. Often, two of my classmates, and my sister, displayed "corny" jokes. It relaxed us in serious situations. We were an advanced and serious group of students and needed the lightheartedness to break the monotony. One solemn occasion when we were being issued books, our instructor directed us to inspect them, then let her know if we found stray marks or writing in them. After inspecting her book, a female classmate got the attention of the instructor by raising her hand:

"Yes", the teacher acknowledged.

The student responded, "Someone has written in my book."

"Who wrote in your book", inquired the teacher.

"The author", exclaimed the student.

In a serious class where students welcomed the release, laughter erupted from all– including the instructor. Though the examples I gave may be tagged inappropriate behavior, "We had no right to interrupt service or class." We were youth doing what youth do; without any signs of environmental stress. As adults, periodically, take time out for some good belly laughter. Sore stomach muscles from laughter may cause you to laugh later when you need it most, just by remembering what caused the soreness. (i.e. Times when you are in meetings and you need a mental escape to think of something less serious, it's OK to laugh.) Laughing has many benefits. Research proves that laughing releases endorphins – the feel good hormone – which promotes an overall sense of well being.

As a society, we have become accustomed to picking and choosing, and have emphasized the right of individuals, until we bring that attitude everywhere we go; including our spiritual life. Many sit in church with spiritual vending machine attitudes; as pressing buttons, then picking and choosing what to respond to and what to reject. Sovereignly choosing what to do with the Word: instead of letting the Word of a Sovereign God choose what they should do. The Word of my have the assurance that He knows you, that joy and peace is called GLORY! When it appears that the Vending Machine is not working properly, or you are not getting out of it what you expected, stop shaking, rocking, punching, kicking, or charging into the machine. Check what you put into it. Did you put in Prayer, and the Fruit of the Spirit? Wait on the Lord. The Word tells us, "If ye shall ask, anything in my name, I will do it" (John 14:14). "What things so ever you desire when you pray, believe that you receive them, and you shall have them" (Mark 11:24). Sometimes, it is not what comes out that matters, it is what went in; it is not always the results, but the motive.

What was your motive for entering the "Break Room"? To unmask, PEEL and have true joy revealed. Often, we do not examine ourselves. Pray and meditate about your emotions. This may cause your joy and laughter to return and remain full. Remember, it's a process. Something to assist in this shift is to change your vocabulary. Labels are given to emotions erroneously. Feelings of discomfort are labeled as anger (mad is not a human emotion). Begin to choose other words to correctly identify the emotion which you are dealing with, specifically. Here is a list from *A* to *Z* to get you started:

*afraid, annoyed, anxious, ashamed, confused, depressed, disappointed, discouraged, disgusted, dissatisfied, embarrassed, envious, frightened, frustrated, gloomy, grumpy, guilty, hateful, hurt, irritated, jealous, left-out, lonesome, miserable, nervous, sad, seared, sorry, tense, terrified, troubled, threatened, unloved, unwanted, worried.*

When emotions are correctly identified and communicated, that is major in the process to finding a resolution. Meditating is valuable, but it is helpful to incorporate a Journal. Feelings of discomfort may bring about imbalances. But writing releases "feel good" hormones. So write about the discomforts or feelings whenever a trigger (root or cause) occurs.

In addition, it is beneficial to change your vocabulary by practicing using positive words to describe your emotions or feelings. Your response to "How are you?" becomes:

*amazing, astonishing, awesome, breathtaking, brilliant, dramatic, electrifying, enlightening, excellent, exceptional, exciting, exquisite, extraordinary, fantastic, flawless, four-star, glorious, handsome, happy, healthy, illustrious, impassioned, impressive, incomparable, inspiring, majestic, magnificent, masterful, mind-blowing, mind-boggling, momentous, optimal, passionate, peerless, powerful, penultimate, perfect, pure, genius, profound, priceless, promising, progressive, provocative, resounding, remarkable, sensational, super, splendid, thrilling, tremendous, unequaled, unstoppable, wonderful, world-class, zestful.*

Emerging from your "Break Room", you've experienced a shift, you are in search of meaningful experiences which will create joy and laughter in your life. Remember, don't sweat the small stuff, but make every life event count. Now, rather than dreading to plan a coming event, you look forward to it with positively great expectations. Equipped with tools for your "joy to return and remain full", your lifetime events become natural highs for you. Create an atmosphere of joy and laughter; look for things to make you smile. Some family and individual activities which may bring laughter to life are:

**REASONS TO LAUGH**

*Dancing, meditation, 5K race, slumber party, a new hobby, swimming the last lap, Christmas Carols, decorating a Christmas Tree, praying, a phone call from a friend that you have not talked with in a while, good grades, skiing, a hug, watching the sunset, family dinners, team winning, a youth's laughter, intercepting a pass, eating pizza, eating holiday dinner, a relaxing bath, hot shower, fellowship, a great book, reading under a comforter on a rainy day, photography, international travel, travel, Chicago Hot Dogs, a great idea, attending sports events, enthusiastic people, climbing trees, celebrating calendar events, God, watching the moon, running, cartoons, making someone laugh, cooking and eating cabbage, loving family, quiet after snowfall, playing an instrument, job well done, friends, singing, concerts, cooking, the first day of school, losing weight, laughter, hearing somebody say, "I love you.", breakfast in bed, loving self, holding hands, fixing something that has been broken, being creative, capturing memories "just because".*

**PEEL** LAUGH LEAD LEARN and LIVE LOVINGLY

# REMEMBER TO LAUGH

𝐿     Love yourself

𝒜     Affirm with positive words

𝒰     Uniqueness is a gift

𝒢     Generosity is for you, too

ℋ     Help yourself to fun!

# CHAPTER 2
# **LEAD**
## Positioned for Leadership

"Leaders identify themselves early in life."

*J*esus was an intentional leader. People followed Him because of the miraculous signs. No doubt, some of his followers were present when Jesus multiplied the wine to meet the needs of all. "And this he said to prove him; for he himself knew what he would do." (John 6:6). Being omniscient God, he knew he was able to do what needed to be done; yet, he was willing to test the faith of his apostles. When you know your gifts, you don't hide them under bushels.

Are your leading in full capacity according to your gifts? As a former classroom teacher, it was important to me to help my students realize their full potential. Often, my classroom management operated as a corporation with the students as stakeholders. Success was eminent mainly because of three things: *Expectations, Rewards, and Consequences.* Expectations (Guidelines) for success in all areas were clarified initially. As the instructional leader, I communicated and demonstrated what was expected of stakeholders (students) to follow. When the stakeholders met expectations, they received favorable results (Rewards). If expectations were not met, the results were not so favorable (Consequences).

When the school year ended, often, I received thank you gifts from students and parents. I fondly recall portions of an enclosed letter which I received with a gift:

"I always admired the way you were able to change the climate of a room, simply by entering it. Without one word from you, all students would immediately return to what was expected. That is the type of teacher I want to be someday." (Of course, I am boohooing at this point; I had no idea of the long term impression).

Teachers (and other professionals) do not always have the privilege of knowing the long term effects they may have on others. Years would pass before I crossed paths with this student again. But I was elated during a chance meeting when the same student shared that he became an educator, and was voted Teacher of the Year by his peers. As a teacher, I did more than demonstrate my abilities, but it was my job to help students' gifts surface. Would you like to bring to surface dormant gifts? According to a leading theorist, Howard Gardner,* there are Multiple Intelligences. Most individuals are familiar with one. For a deeper understanding, please research this topic. I will highlight major traits of each.

## THE NINE TYPES OF INTELLIGENCES*

**Naturalist** (Nature Smart) The ability to discriminate among living things as well as other natural features. Examples: Farmers, Botanists, Chefs, etc.

**Musical Intelligence** (Musical Smart) The ability to recognize, create, reproduce, and reflect on music. There is a connection between music and the emotions. Young adults dominant in this intelligence are usually singing or drumming to themselves, and are aware of sounds that others may miss. Musical Intelligence is demonstrated through composers, conductors, musicians, vocalists, artists, and sensitive listeners.

**Logical-Mathematical Intelligence** (Reasoning and Numbers Smart) This intelligence is characterized by the ability to perceive relationships and connections in order to use abstract and symbolic thoughts. Also, they are able to calculate, quantify, consider propositions and hypotheses, and carry out mathematical operations. These individuals may be interested in patterns, categories, strategy games, and experiments. Examples: Engineers, Scientists, Architects.

**Existential Intelligence** (Philosophically Smart) The ability to locate self with respect to human existence and conditions. This deals with the profound experiences such as love of others, and the sensitivity to tackle deep questions about human existence and life: Who are we? What's it all about? Why is there evil? Where is humanity heading? Is there meaning in life? These questions and others are often pondered by pastors, theologians, priests, ministers, philosophers, scientists, writers, artists, etc.

**Interpersonal Intelligence** (People Smart) Individuals with this intelligence as dominant are your born leaders. This is the ability to understand and interact effectively with others, sensitivity to the moods and temperaments, and the ability to entertain multiple perspectives. Teachers, counselors, social workers, actors, and politicians are some professionals exhibiting this intelligence.

**Bodily-Kinesthetic** (Body Smart) People dominant in this intelligence are skilled in using their body to convey feelings and ideas. They have good hand-eye coordination and are very aware of their bodies. Their fine and gross motor complete, use the results and focus on the dominant traits. It would be a great injustice to attempt to enlighten the shadow traits. (Usually, the shadow or less dominant traits will increase as the dominant traits are mobilized or enriched). *The Multiple Intelligences* Inventory is an extremely helpful tool to assist in understanding leadership styles of others as well as your own. "Followship" flows smoother with a better understanding of leadership. In addition to leadership styles, the requirements for effective leaders must be met.

## Requirements for Effective Leaders

"After the death of Moses, the Lord's disciple, God spoke to Moses assistant, whose name was Joshua (the son of Nun). Now that my disciple is dead, you are the new leader of Israel. Lead my people across the Jordan River into the Promised Land. I say to you what I said to Moses: Wherever you go will be part of the land of Israel – all the way from Negeb desert in the south to the Lebanon Mountains in the north, and from the Mediterranean Sea in the west to the Euphrates River in the east; including all the land of the Hittites. No one will be able to oppose you as long as long as you live, for I will be with you just as I am with Moses. I will not abandon you or fail to help you. Be strong and brave for you will be a successful leader of my people, and they shall

conquer all the land I promised to their ancestors. You need only to be strong and courageous and to obey to the letter every law Moses gave you, for if you are careful to obey every one of them, you will be successful in everything you do. Constantly remind the people about these laws, and you yourself must think about them every day and every night so that you will be sure to obey all of them. For only then will you succeed. Yes, be bold and strong! Banish fear and doubt! For remember, the Lord your God is with you wherever you go." Joshua 1: 1-9

    Before Moses died, the Lord pointed out to him the promised land. The Lord said, "I promised Abraham, Isaac, and Jacob that I would give it to their descendants. Now, you have seen it, but you will not enter it." After the death of Moses, the leadership of a nation fell on Joshua. God is true to His promises. He promised His people a land and they are now entering in to possess it. However, it was not automatic; God required of them that they actively engage in warfare in order to gain what he had given them. Take heed: Before asking the Lord, "Why me?", ask yourself, "Have I met all of the requirements of the Lord?"

    Well, Joshua mobilized his forces and prepared them for battle. After this, they crossed the Jordan River and the battle began. It was on! Joshua's example is one of an effective leader. Effective leaders must know whose and who they are; as well as embody the following characteristics:

DEFINED – a leader is one who possesses the Spirit of Christ and has the heart of a server. To be a leader requires great love, honor, tolerance, watchfulness, prayers, intercession, and unquestioning obedience. Leaders are chosen by God, yet, trained by the officer he/she would serve. Also, one who stands beside the leader, assists him/her, lifts them up, and protects them against any enemy who might attempt to attack them. Leaders are required to have teachable spirits, and should be teachers, themselves. This allows them to develop others and receive development.

DEVELOPED – You will never arrive at a place where you will not need to submit to anyone. Jesus developed the twelve disciples by placing a portion of himself into them. Leadership is developed by studying under an effective leader. It is not your education or the amount of hours you spend on an assignment. It is all about the time spent with the Lord, and modeling effective leadership.

DEDICATED – True dedication is making decisions based on a commitment to God, not on feelings or emotions. A leader being developed, such as Joshua, is one who is dedicated to his/her leader to:

- Provide strength to his/her leader.
- Have a deep sense of respect for the leader's way of doing things.

- Instinctively understand the leader's thoughts.
- Walk in submission to the leader.
- Work toward the advancement of common goals.
- Force onward, without giving out under what you think to be harsh treatment.
- Follow directions.
- Support leaders.
- Communicate with excellence. This does not only refer to diction, pronunciation, enunciation, or syllabication; but it refers to being persistent and consistent with the Word of God!
- Gain victories for the leader, eagerly.
- Encourage others, and endure to the end of assignment.

DETERMINED – Instead of offering ourselves to wait on others, we expect others to wait on us. Leaders, at time, need the tenacity of a bear but be as gentle as a lamb. Once determined toward a cause, the leader begins to lead a more disciplined life.

DISCIPLINED – Leaders purpose to lead disciplined lifestyles in every area of life; including but not limited to controlling your tongue, time management, eating habits, exercise, etc. Additional public disciplines should include:

- Having a commitment and faithfulness to assignments.
- Demonstrating loyalty to family.
- Showing a genuine interest in people of all types.
- Avoiding complaining and murmuring.
- Being a good listener.
- Being optimistic.

Leading a lifestyle of discipline, precedes the natural progression of taking care of one's assignments and duties.

DUTIES – It is imperative for a leader to keep an open mind, and remain receptive to endless opportunities. Following is a summarized list of duties and responsibilities. A leader should:

- Accept his/her position with honor.
- Have a respect for team members.
- Follow directions immediately, and correctly.
- Practice excellent communication skills.
- Be an encourager.

Finally, a leader is the person responsible for the order of the group; therefore, by whatever means necessary, the leader should guide the group in coming to a consensus, or provide an established set of expectations or guidelines to follow. Study this example:

**DIRECTIONS** – guidelines for a healthy group

*Explain* the concept of Reciprocity.
*Set* the standards for proper behavior.
*Establish* safety.
One person talks at a time.
*Be courteous*. Listen to the person talking.
*Use confidentiality*. Do not discuss group's details with anyone else.
*Show respect*: No bullying, put downs, or teasing.
*Set* a positive tone for dialogue.
*Create* consensus.
*Set* goals / or develop a mission statement.
*Encourage* esprit de corps.

As an effective leader, the expectations and guidelines for your group must be established in love. Incorporating love with your expectations translate three ways:

**Involve**: Give all stakeholders opportunities to have input during the formative stage.

**Empower**: Encourage active participation with Leadership responsibilities.

**Appreciate**: Acknowledge presence with validation; whether verbal or tangible.

If you are waiting on a pat on the back, you may be operating out of the realm of your gift. Remember, we are entrusted with gifts to carry out God's plan and there is only one right way to carry it out. God's way.

# CHAPTER 3
# **LEARN**
## Charge Your Atmosphere

"Focus on your strengths"

*H*ow a person learns, largely depends on interactions, engagement, and day to day activities. Explore and clarify individual learning styles to be incorporated into daily, life. Though we are uniquely and wonderfully formed, our commonalities outweigh our differences – which set us apart from others. Interactions may be observed mainly in the following ways:

**Kinesthetic** – the ability or need to move, touch, or form to assist in the learning process. (Models; Projects)

**Visual** – the ability to learn by viewing print rich materials. (Books; Posters; Role-Playing)

**Auditory** – the ability to absorb knowledge based on hearing. (Lectures; Music)

As a learner, focus on the style which impacts you, most. Use ingenious methods to get your point across to other, and to help you to retain information. Rhythm, rhyme, acronyms, and mnemonic devices should be incorporated as helpful learning tools. A mnemonic device which was Holy Ghost inspired and created has proven to be extremely effective in this process:

*COMMUNICATE* –   Speak with clarity and always give a good report.  Avoid allowing foul words to enter your mouth or spirit. "And these words which I command you today shall be in your heart.  You shall talk of them diligently to your youth, and shall talk of them when you sit in your house, when you walk by the way, when you lie down, and when you rise up." (Deuteronomy 6: 6,7). Learners must acquire excellent verbal skills, but they must also set good examples.

*DEMONSTRATE* – You are never alone; someone is always watching you. Whether or not you raised your hand for the job, you are a role model.  When the Church at Corinth went away from the things of God, Paul went to warn them of idolatry and sin.  "Imitate me, just as I also imitate Christ."  (1 Corinthians 11:1).  Followers or students soak up attitudes as if they are sponges. Paul recognized the importance of this.

*FACILITATE* – Once you have been guided through the process, you will be held accountable for following the right path.  "Train up a youth in the way he should go, and when he is old he will not depart from it." (Proverbs 22:6).  The opportunity will present itself for learners to apply what they have heard and seen. As a learner, you must always be ready to be an effective witness. The world needs to see that you are different; that you have something that they do not have. But you must be willing to nurture them and show them the way to a more abundant life.

NURTURING OTHERS

Often, leaders are not sure which direction to point their followers because they are not sure of their own direction. It is possible that they are going in an unlikely direction. However, teach; not condemn, when a follower or student sees another doing the wrong thing.

People do the things they do because of *personality* or *temperament*. (a person's nature as it controls the way he or she feels, behaves or thinks). Personalities may be classified into four temperament types with animal symbolism. (according to Smalley and Trent):

*Melancholic* (a wise and quiet **beaver**). Go getter; Strong sense of right and wrong. Things are pretty much black and white for this personality type. Very emotional; creative; constructive.

*Phlegmatic* (a relaxed and peaceful **golden retriever**). Fetch what you need and will stick by you, even in the rain. Has a desire to serve to make your load easier.

*Sanguine* (an enthusiastic and active **otter**). Playful, fun-loving, life of the party, and trendsetter. Likes everyone and everyone loves them.

*Choleric* (a short tempered and fast **lion**). Ruler of things and strong-willed. His or her way is the right way.

    We can all be as diamonds in the rough. There are numerous forces which impact lives; therefore, they impact learning. Pray and ask the Lord to reveal to you your most effective relationship and learning style. The Lord can polish and smooth rough places so that we may be used for His purpose in a more excellent way. Get well acquainted with these rough places or forces.

    Overexposure to life situations can have powerful and often times damaging effect on the individuals; especially youth. This may be extended through adulthood when left unattended. It can leave individuals traumatized without anyone realizing there has been an exposure to trauma. Exposure to trauma can, in turn, have a profound effect on behavior and the ability to function successfully. To lead a healthy lifestyle, it helps to recognize the signs and symptoms of trauma. But before we identify the symptoms, the forces in our day -to-day environment will be described:


FORCES THAT IMPACT LEARNING
(Life Situations)

**Adult Situations** – Either through real life circumstances or through the media, youth are frequently faced with adult situations, which require the mature mental and emotional capacities to process and understand. Many youth spend a great deal of their lives (especially in the Summer months) in front of the television. Consequently, they are exposed to every imaginable, and unimaginable, aspect of human behavior, while they are unable to make judgments about what they see. Statistics have proven that the typical youth watching 27 hours of TV per week will view 8,000 murders, and 100,000 acts of violence from age 3 to 12.

**Conflicting Values** – Values and morals which used to be passed down by family and community members, are now presented to youth through media, as well. This means that youth are exposed to many different ideas of right, wrong, good, and bad. Exposure to multiple value systems can be enriching for adults, but confusing and perplexing to youth. This leaves them to try to figure out these powerful issues on their own.

**Trauma and Loss** – More youth than ever have experienced the loss of a parent through death or divorce. Even in the best circumstances, divorces can leave youth feeling many confusing and upsetting emotions. More youth than not are living in non-traditional families. They have experienced the pain of loss of a much-loved parent in their daily lives or, in worse cases, they have experienced severe trauma as one parent makes the decision to divorce an abusive spouse. Various other forms of trauma affect youth's lives as can be seen by the rising incidence of youth abuse and adolescent suicide.

**Violence and Brutality** – Research has shown that hearing and seeing a message presented strongly and repeatedly will influence the viewer to go out and buy the product. TV programs are paid for by advertisers. Today's youth can turn on the TV at any hour of the day or night and witness acts of violence and brutality. Well, does it not follow that repeated exposure to violence and brutality will also influence behavior? We must stop saying, "In my day . . ." because many of us grew up without witnessing brutality in our homes through TV. The most violence we saw on TV came from the cartoons; such as, the Road Runner, Bugs Bunny and the like.

**Life Altering/Threatening Decisions** – Even Elementary School youth are being faced with choices about drug use and sexual activity; both of which can be life destroying. How dreadful to have to make life and death decisions without the benefit of maturity, wisdom, or experience. Many who say, "In my day . . . " never had to face such frightening choices in their day.

**Negative and Disrespectful Adults** – Too often, it is difficult for youth to find positive adult role models. Youth without positive role models in their families are especially vulnerable. Even at the highest levels of our society, adults can be seen and heard (again, I emphasize, via the media) to speak and act disrespectfully and without honor. Youth have always been witnesses to bad adult behavior, but never on the scale they now experience.

**Noise and Stimulation** – We live in a very noisy world. We think nothing of the lack of silence, or of peace and quiet. Youth are exposed to constant stimulation. Some spent the vast majority of their lives in front of the media. They have little time to think, imagine and daydream. All this is done for them through media.

**Environmental Toxins** – While every effort is made to protect youth from environmental toxins, today's youth are growing up in a world environmentally very different from the one in which their parents and grandparents lived as youth. It is easy to forget that whatever toxins are present in the environment, they impact youth more than they do adults – if for no other reason, its because of size. How this phenomenon influences the behavior of youth is still unknown. Again, the "In my day . . . " group did not grow up in a day when their parents even heard of environmental toxins, more or less had to be concerned for them.

Exposure to trauma can, have a profound effect on behavior and ability to function successfully. To work effectively with youth, it helps to recognize the signs and symptoms of trauma:

## FIVE IMPACTING SYMPTOMS OF OVEREXPOSURE TO TRAUMATIC FORCES

Responses after being traumatized

DISASSOCIATION – is the same as being distracted or daydreaming; except, taking it to the extreme level.

INAPPROPRIATE REACTION – often the reactions do not fit the situation. When a person becomes highly reactive to a minor irritation.

HYPERSENSITIVITY – (similar to IR) not always emotional. It includes things such as, light, noise, touch, tone of voice, colors, closed in places, or anything that may unconsciously remind them of previous trauma.

INEFFECTIVE COGNITIVE PROCESSING – acts on impulse. They can't always think at the moment they are feeling an intense emotion.

Think of the last time you were irritated -with an adult. You were probably able to think of consequences, then made a good decision about what you were going to say or do. Traumatized individuals; especially youth, can't do that.

NO CONCEPT OF FUTURE – The entire U. S. Educational System is based on the concept of future, and most traditional discipline methods are based on the ability to perceive future consequences for here-and-now behavior. After being overexposed to trauma, individuals; especially youth, cannot conceptualize themselves at a different age or time in their lives. The "here and now" is all that is real to them. (Often, they suffer from PTSD – Post Traumatic Stress Disorder).

## DEFENSE MECHANISMS

The mind is a very complex unit. Whenever anxiety occurs, the mind first responds by an increase in problem-solving thinking, seeking ways of escaping the situation. When this is not successful, defense mechanisms may be triggered. They help individuals cope with anxiety and prevent the *ego* (how a person feels about them<u>selves:</u> confidence, respect, esteem, worth or importance) from being overwhelmed.

Defense mechanisms may result in healthy or unhealthy consequences depending on the circumstance and frequency with which they are used. They may be viewed as normal behavior; rather than being *pathological* (hardened, obsessive, senile, habitual, or compulsive), and may have adaptive value as long as these behaviors do not become a lifestyle. When employing mechanisms as part of their normal behavior, it enables individuals to avoid facing reality. However, mechanisms may reduce anxiety arising from unacceptable or harmful events. During research from different scientists, it was found that mechanisms are categorized in a variety of ways. For sake of discussion, this chapter categorizes them as mature and immature.

**Mature Defense Mechanisms:**

Acceptance – The ability to recognize a process or condition without attempting to change it, protest, or exit because a situation is disliked. (Or when great risk or cost may be associated with change).

Courage – The willingness to confront conflicts, fear, pain, obstacles, intimidation, or uncertainty. Moral courage deals with ideals of fairness and justice; while physical courage often extends lives.

Emotional self-regulation - The ability to respond to experiences by modifying the type, duration, intensity, or expression of various emotions.

Emotional self-sufficiency – The ability to self-affirm or self-validate. Not dependent on approval or disapproval of others.

Forgiveness – The ability to cease resentment or demanding retribution or restitution as a result of a perceived offense, disagreement, or mistake.

Gratitude – The ability to feel thankfulness or appreciation of a wide range of people and events. Gratitude may be credited for and associated with higher levels of happiness and lower levels of depression and stress.

Humility – The ability to use intelligent self-respect which prevents thinking too highly or too lowly of oneself by considering one's imperfections.

Identification – The ability to model another person's character and behavior.

Mercy – The ability to show compassion for others.

Mindfulness – The ability to adopt an attitude of acceptance, curiosity, and openness toward experiences.

Moderation – The ability to exercise self-restraint by staying within reasonable limits of desires.

Patience – The willingness to endure difficult circumstances; such as, delay, criticism, attack, or provocation, to prevent responding negatively. Patience is a virtue.

Respect – The willingness to show appreciation because of specific feelings regarding qualities of a person. Contacts or relationships without respect are seldom long term. The lack of respect is at the very heart of most conflict in families, communities, and nations.

Tolerance – The ability to deliberately practice allowing behavior which is low on your list of approval.

## Immature Defense Mechanisms

Compensation - Consists of masking perceived weaknesses or developing certain positive traits to make up for limitations. This mechanism can have direct adjustive value, and it may also be an attempt by the person to say, "Don't see the ways in which I am inferior, but see me in my accomplishments."

Denial – Plays a defensive role. It generally operates at preconscious and conscious levels. Denial of reality is perhaps the simplest of all self-defense mechanisms. It is a way of distorting what the individual thinks, feels, or perceives in a traumatic situation. It consists of defending against anxiety by "closing one's eyes" to the existence of threatening reality.

Displacement – Consists of directing energy toward another object or person when the original object or person is inaccessible. This is described as coping with anxiety by shifting impulses from a threatening object to a safer target. For example: An individual who feels intimidated by their boss comes home and unloads hostility on much younger, smaller, or safer targets – youth.

Identification – (This may also appear in the developmental process as mature). Identification may enhance self-worth and protect one from a sense of being a failure. Individuals who basically feel inferior may identify themselves with successful causes, organizations, or people in the hope that they will be perceived as worthwhile.

Introjection – Consists of taking on the principles, values, or standards of others as one's own. For example: Often captives deal with overwhelming anxiety by accepting the values of the enemy to gain the enemy's approval.

Projection - Consists of attributing to others one's own unacceptable desires and impulses. For example: "Those people, not me" are lustful, aggressive, etc.

Rationalization – Helps to justify specific behavior patterns, and softens the blow of disappointments. For example: When a position applied for is not attained, the individual may convince themselves that they did not want the position, anyway. Thus, manufacturing reasons to explain a bruised ego.

Reaction Formation – Individuals may conceal hate with a façade of love, be extremely nice when they harbor negative reactions, or mask cruelty with excessive kindness.

Regression – To go back to an earlier phase of development when there were fewer demands. In the face of severe stress or challenge, youth who are frightened in school may return to weeping, or clinging to the teacher.

Repression – May be explained as an involuntary removal of something from consciousness. It is assumed that most of the painful events of the first 5 or 6 years of life are buried, but these events later influence behavior. It is a disorder which painful thoughts are excluded from awareness.

Ritual / Undoing – A person tries to undo an unhealthy, destructive or threatening thought or action by engaging in contrary behavior.

Sublimation – Diverting aggressive energy into other channels;   channels are usually socially acceptable and often times, admirable. For example, aggressive impulses can be channeled into athletic activities, so that the person finds a way of expressing emotions and is often praised.

## Summary of Immature Defense Mechanisms

| 1 | Compensation: Strengthen one to hide another. |
|---|---|
| 2 | Denial: Refuse to face a negative behavior |
| 3 | Displacement: Take it out on someone else. |
| 4 | Identification: Attach to something positive. |
| 5 | Introjection: Conform feelings for approval. |
| 6 | Projection: See your faults in others. |
| 7 | Rationalization: Excuse and justify mistakes. |
| 8 | Reaction Formation: Pretend you are different. |
| 9 | Regression: Act much younger to feel better. |
| 10 | Repression: Putting things into darkness. |
| 11 | Ritual and Undoing: Override negative with habit. |
| 12 | Sublimation: Divert negative into acceptable. |

## LEARN TO LISTEN

Active listening is a vital part of effective communication. With active listening, judgment is suspended and the listener uses empathy to try to understand the speaker's experience, feelings, and point of view. Components of active listening are:

*Encourage* - Use nonverbal and verbal cues to show the other person that you are really listening. Example: Use body language and short but vocal responses. (Note: These change across cultures.)

*Paraphrase* – Repeat what the speaker said. This shows you are listening, and helps fact-check.
Example: "He said he would call right back and the didn't."
"You're saying that you felt hurt when he didn't call back."

*Clarify* – Ask questions to confirm what the speaker has said. Not only will this help you understand, but it may help the speaker examine his or her own perceptions.
Example: "I'm still not sure I understand why that made you angry. Could you explain once more."

*Reflect* – State what you think the speaker is experiencing. This may lead the speaker to be more expressive. It also provides a way to check the accuracy of your perception.
Example: "You sound upset; It seems as if you still feel hurt".

*Summarize* – Major ideas, themes, and feelings are repeated. This continues dialogue.
Example: "The main problem(s) you have with this is . . ."

*Validate* – Reaffirm your positive feelings about being part of the dialogue. Show appreciation for the speaker's efforts.
Example: "I'm happy that we are talking."

*Refrain from Judging* - Dismiss the urge to give suggestions. The speaker may feel patronized or attacked.
Example: Do not say: "It's no big deal; why are you upset?" "I think you should just forget him!"

Communication is far more than speaking; it is also active listening and hearing. There are a variety of key elements to keep communications open; and not blocked. To enhance your skills, practice identifying, then eradicating these inappropriate blockers from discussions:

## COMMUNICATION BLOCKERS

*Accusing*
"I'm not sure I'm college material. I don't think I'll do well.'
"Don't be silly. Of course you'll do well.

*Globalizing*
"Can we see a different movie? I don't like science fiction."
"No matter what I suggest, you always want to do something else!"

*Ignoring*
"You won't believe what happened to me in Gym Class!"
"Oh yeah? Just listen to what happened to me."

*Insulting*
"How was your day? Flunk any tests?"

*Interrupting*
"Why don't we –
"Forget it. We need *good* ideas."

*Name-Calling*
"Hey, that's my job."
"Forget it, jerk. Why are you so possessive and uptight?"

*Sarcasm*
"For once in your life, could you clean this room?"

*Stating opinion as fact*
"The Blues had a really bad season."
"The Blues are the worst team on the face of the earth."

*Word usage / disregard for language*

"The mens need to stop taking everything personal."

**PLAY THAT BACK**
    Words take on different meanings with changes in tone of voice, body language, and facial expressions. Each of the following sentences may be read several ways. Alone, or with a partner, practice new ways to say one sentence. Continue with the same sentence until no one can think of more ways to say it. Then continue to a different sentence:

Pass me the book.
Glenn will be at the party.
Where is my hat?
She has to be home by 11.
Why can't you come with us?
I'll talk to you later.
You're my friend, right?
What a week I've had.
Give me a bite of your cake.
The boss wants to see you.
What do you want?
Where is it?
I'm taking care of the babies today.
What's going on?

## CHARGE YOUR ATMOSPHERE

Begin to make a difference in your environment by being assertive, and letting people around you know when and how you would like them to change their behavior. "I" messages allow you to do this without using blame or put downs. However, there may be pitfalls to avoid in the suggested plan for action. For example: It is not mandatory to follow my suggested parts or steps in order. The scenario will dictate whether it is more appropriate to begin with "When you" and not "I feel". Note: Avoid disguising an accusation, blame, put down, or an insult as an "I" message.

"I" messages create a positive atmosphere for communication and problem solving. There are four main parts to follow for an "I" message:

"I feel (state the feeling/ emotion)"
"I feel disappointed and hurt".

"When you (state the other person's behavior)... when you repeat something that I asked you not to repeat.

"Because (state the effect on you): Because it is embarrassing?

Because it is embarrassing, and it made other people angry at me.

I want (state what you want to happen)
I want you to keep your promises to me.

When stating the "I feel" part of the message, always name a feeling. Make extra efforts to send positive "I" messages, also. "I'm really excited about you completing your assignments. It makes me feel that you care about this project."

"Enjoy learning; learning to enjoy."

# CHAPTER 4
# LIVE
## Take Care of You, Totally

"Enjoy what you have rather than desiring what you don't have".
(Ecclesiastes 6:9 NIV)

*A*n important variable in life is to live by minimizing the stress levels in your life. It is often easier said than done, but once the decision is made, you must consistently and persistently pursue your plan, in order to execute it for success. Here is the plan:

Accept that you cannot give attention to everything. Your first step in effectively alleviating stress is to dismiss this exaggerated sense of what you should be able to process. Accept: There is too much information for you to handle! Now that we've cleared that up, you need to chillax and deal with the reality of living in a world packed with attention demands. A word synonymous with plan is *goal*. When pursuing *goals*, it is always in order to create a guide to assist you with navigating your plan/*goal*. This is termed *goal setting*. Goals should be further categorized as: short term (**weekly**), intermediate (**monthly**), or long range (**annually**). Each category should specifically address the following questions and more:

**Goals**

What? (What do I desire to accomplish?)
When? (When should it materialize?)

How? (How will I change my actions for results?) Who? (Who may I depend on for support?)

*Make prioritizing a priority.* Your first priority should be to take a little undisturbed time each day to evaluate the various demands on your attention before they show up. Do your prioritizing whenever you typically think most clearly. Most people do best in the morning, but I like to take fifteen minutes before I go to bed to preview the upcoming day. Rank your tasks in order of importance and write them down.

PEEL some things from your list by making healthy lifestyle changes with food, events, exercise, people, etc. When you are being hounded for attention, you will have the following acronym as a visual cue to help you focus on the most significant tasks, first. Leave less necessary or minor items for later – or for *never*:

**P** = *Pray Powerfully*
**E** = *Eat Efficiently*
**E** = *Exercise Enthusiastically*
**L** = *Laugh, Lead, Learn, & Live Lovingly*

Plan with purpose. Consider each task on your *goals* "to-do" list with these two questions in mind. If a "to-do" item does not serve either purpose, it has to go!
Questions:

What experiences do I want to have during my time on this Earth?

How do I want the world to be different (because in large ways or small, it will be different) because I have lived?

*Designate a period of time*.  Get into a frame of mind to designate a period of time during which you will focus entirely on a given activity.  The session should not be long – half an hour is a good start.  Be sure to set a timer as a reminder to sound when your work session is finished.  Put the timer where you cannot see it; pushing you to devote all attention to the task at hand.  You *should* notice an increase in productivity.  (Vision Boards are great measuring tools!)

*Back off for a while*.  If you feel overwhelmed, take a break for a while.  Being overwhelmed is as being in a swimming pool drowning when it is not necessary to drown.  "STAND-UP!"  It's not that deep! (Pun intended).  If you've lost your life's true passion to be productive, don't beat yourself up.  Back off for a while, but don't go idle, either.  Just try something different; something you don't care about *as much*.  At the very least, it will keep you pleasantly distracted while life sorts itself out. Before you realize what is happening, it may have led you safely all the way home – back to your passion.

*Give yourself permission to be still.* Write into your schedule a time for meditation and prayer. You need a time for quietness and free of distractions. Take time to hear from God, daily.

*Adopt positive affirmations.* Recognize that it is your feelings and your thoughts that make you feel pressured, not the tasks you have to complete. They will get done – or not; and you and the world will survive. Even if you do have a crucial deadline, you will have a much better chance of making it if you feel "relaxed", and can proceed with a calm mind. Feeling frantic will not make you more efficient. On the contrary, it encourages mistakes and glitches. Sometimes just a phrase may help. Have a self-talk:
Repeat, "I declare I am relaxed, I have successfully completed my assignment". Plan affirmations which are appropriate for your day-to-day schedule. Take care of you! Following is an excerpt from my book, PEEL EAT EFFCIENTLY. I am passionate about seeing God's people take authority over their lives, totally:

**PEEL** LAUGH LEAD LEARN and LIVE LOVINGLY

## TAKE CARE OF YOUR TOTAL BEING

Guard your gates. The benefits to taking care of your Spiritual Health, what you place in your body, how much your body is at rest, and who you allow in your personal space - may have significantly positive or negative effects on your health. There are multiple dynamics to our lives. (We are spirit, soul, and body). However, when we follow the commands of our Lord and Savior, we enjoy a peace and joy unspeakable in every area of life; this is "*Living*". Whatever, the Lord tells you to do; do it. I actually struggled with including the following section. I struggled was "masked" in which "L" will I place it with, etc. The truth is, Evangelism encompasses "L5" all.

### Evangelism

Jesus spoke to his disciples saying, "…Go therefore and make disciples of all… teaching them to observe all things that I have commanded you…" (Matthew 28: 18-20). This is known as the *Great Commission*. Everything we do should contribute to fulfilling this commission. There are five major parts:

1. Evangelism - We must win people out of the world. God's plan for evangelizing the world is for Christians to share the gospel with the lost. Christians must "speak, live, and show His good news of salvation to persons separated from Him".
2. Discipleship – A disciple is a mature follower of Christ. Christian maturity requires personal holiness, ethical living, fervent witnessing, and characteristics that Jesus commanded of his disciples.
3. Ministry – Ministry is meeting another person's needs in the name of Jesus. It involves helping people both inside and outside of the church. It places us in contact with people who have physical and emotional needs. When believers exercise their gifts, needs are met and Christ is glorified.
4. Fellowship – involves more than refreshments. It involves the personal relationships developed through the open-hearted sharing of life's joys and sorrows. People need to be known by name and missed when they are

Apples suppress the appetite without robbing the body of necessary nutrients, so they are great for dieters.

Natural juices in apples are highly effective virus fighters.

They lower both bad cholesterol and high blood pressure.

They help stabilize blood sugar; important factor in controlling diabetes.

Apples help prevent constipation, or help treat diarrhea.

They prevent tooth decay.

They contain chemicals that scientists believe are vital in stopping cancer.

According to researched studies, apples will keep you healthy for a longer period of time. Listed are a few of the various ways: Apples –

*Regulate your day* – You do not have to be concerned about being regular anymore. Whether your problem is visiting the bathroom too often or not often enough, apples can help. One apple with its skin contains four to five grams of fiber – the most important nutrient in keeping your bowels working like a well-oiled machine.

Keeping yourself regular without relying on harmful laxatives could be as easy as replacing that afternoon snack of potato chips or cookies with a crisp, delicious apple. Applesauce is actually the best apple product for diarrhea since it is made without the high-five skin.

*Keep your body young* – Many diseases that seem to be a part of aging are kept from you by antioxidants. So many people are taking supplements for protection that it has become a multibillion-dollar industry. A fresh apple has more that fifteen times the antioxidants power of the daily recommended dose of vitamin C.

Research also proves that ordinary apples were able to stop the growth of colon and liver cancer cells in test tubes. Unpeeled apples were especially effective. Why purchase *additional* supplements when you can get better antioxidants firepower from a sweet, crunchy fruit? This is just another "W" question.

*Cut your risk of heart disease* - Sometimes it is hard to remember which food is good for which part of your body. When you pick up your next apple, examine it carefully. It is shaped a bit like a heart – and that should help you
remember apples are good for your heart! It is the magnesium and potassium in apples that help regulate your blood pressure and keep your heart beating steadily. It is a naturally occurring antioxidant, flavonoid quercetin that protects your artery walls from damage and keeps your blood

flowing smoothly.

*Strike at the heart of strokes* – Apples are even a smart choice for helping avoid strokes. The connection is clear – people who regularly eat apples are less likely to have strokes than people who do not.

*Protect your joints* – Few people get arthritis in areas of the world where fruits and vegetables make up a large part of the diet. Apples contain boron, a trace mineral many plants absorb from the soil. Boron is credited in preventing arthritis. You need three to ten milligrams a day to affect your risk of arthritis. It is not reasonable to eat nine apples a day. Try pairing an apple with peanut butter, or raisins.

*Help you breathe deeply* – Air pollution, pollen, cigarette smoke and other air-borne nastiness assault your lungs daily. Besides, you may suffer from asthma, emphysema or a lung condition. Sometimes all you want to do is to take a deep breath. Grab "an apple a day". Unfortunately, apples cannot reverse an existing lung condition, but you can add a line of defense against future damage and alleviate the severity of your symptoms. When purchasing apples, be sure they are not bruised; they are firm and have good color. At home, take them out of their plastic bag and store them in your refrigerator – loose in the produce bin or in a paper bag are best. Apples absorb odors, so keep them away from strong smelling foods such as garlic or onions. Be careful of purchasing cider from a roadside stand; harmful E.coli bacteria could be present in unpasteurized apple juice or cider. Always try to buy organically grown apples (produced without chemicals). If you can not find organically grown apples, either scrub your produce well or sacrifice that fiber-rich peel before eating.

**Other Fruits**

*Bananas* – Aid the muscular and nervous systems – the natural sugars are ready for use as fuel. Also, the banana promotes sleep and contains enzymes that assist in the reproduction of sexual hormones.
*Blackberries* – Relieve diarrhea; an astringent and a tonic.
*Blueberries* – Improve sluggish circulation and benefits the eyesight; especially night vision. They may be used in the treatment of varicose veins, hemorrhoids, and peptic ulcers. They rejuvenate the pancreas and aid in relieving dysentery. Fresh berries help heal mouth infections. Blueberries are laxatives and a blood cleanser.

*Cherries* – Cherries relieve painful urinary infections and stop constant urination. Cherries are well-known remedies for gout, arthritis, and rheumatism. They combat the harmful effects of animal protein, and benefits the liver blood and gallbladder.

*Dates* – Dates were among the most abundant of all fruit of the Holy Land. These sweet fruits grow on palm trees that can be 100 feet high. They grow in clusters with as many as 200 dates per cluster. They can be yellow, orange, red, green, or brown.

*Figs* – Have been prized since ancient times for their sweetness and nutritional value. Greek and Roman athletes ate figs to increase their stamina and improve their performance.

*Grapes* – Grapes with seeds help cut the mucus and catarrh of the body so they can be eliminated. They detoxify the body; especially good for the digestive tract, liver, kidneys and blood. Their simple sugars are absorbed into the bloodstream. Grapes aid in improving anemic conditions.

*Grapefruit* – Aids in the removal or dissolving of inorganic calcium which may have formed deposits in the joints (arthritis for example). It normalizes red blood cells levels. Excellent for the cardiovascular system; helping to lower blood cholesterol. It is a natural antiseptic for wounds and is valuable as a drug or poison eliminator.

*Lemon* – Nourishes the brain and nerve cells. It reduces fevers, destroys putrefactive bacteria in the intestines and mouth and alleviates flatulence and indigestion. Strengthens the body structures and makes for healthy teeth. May be used as a hair rinse or facial astringent.

*Melon* – (Cantaloupe)- Cleanses and rehydrates the body. Rejuvenates and alkalinizes the body. It is used in patients with heart disease to keep the blood thin and to relieve angina attacks; requires no digestion when eaten alone.

*Orange* – Daily use will aid in toning up and purifying the entire system. Aids digestion and stimulates the activity of the
glands in the stomach.

*Raspberries* - Are beneficial for all female organs, they help relieve menstrual cramps, and will decrease the menstrual flow. Good cleanser for mucus and for toxins in the body.

*Strawberries* – Good for the intestinal tract; a cleansing food that rids the blood of harmful toxins. If you rub a clean cut strawberry over the face, it will clear the skin.

*Watermelon* – Alleviates stress and depression. It is a cooling food, and an excellent / detoxifier for the entire body. It is a diuretic. The white rind of the melon is one of the highest organic sodium foods. The outer peel is one of the best sources of chlorophyll. As a diuretic, it quickly flushes the bladder.

## VEGETABLES

In recipes, some vegetables are extremely versatile when used to flavor other dishes. They are delicate and form the basis of many traditional dishes which originated in ancient Israel and neighboring lands. The Bible says that in the earliest days of creation, all of God's creation, even animals were vegetarians. As you read, you will find out when to eat which vegetables and what God designed it to do.

*Asparagus* – Neutralizes excess amounts of ammonia in the body and aids in preventing the rupturing of small blood vessels. Asparagus encourages evacuation of bowels by increasing fecal bulk with undigested fiber. It serves as a blood builder due to its chlorophyll content and contains many of the elements that build the liver, kidneys, skin, ligaments and bones.

*Avocado* – Regulates the body functions and stimulates growth. It aids in red blood regeneration and prevention of nutritional anemia. When used regularly, it will improve hair and skin quality as well as soothe the digestive tract. It contains organic fat and protein.

*Broccoli* – Contains almost as much calcium as whole milk. Benefits rough skin and counteracts the sulphur compounds
that form gas.

*Brussel Sprouts* – Stimulates the liver and other tissues out of stagnancy. They are rich in alkalizing elements with specific affinity for the pancreas. Aids in reducing the risk of cancer; especially colon cancer.

*Cabbage\** – Detoxifies the stomach and upper bowels of waste; therefore, improving digestive efficiency and facilitating rapid elimination. Works to alkalize the body, stimulate the immune system, kill harmful bacteria and viruses, soothe and heal ulcers, reduce the risk of cancer, and clear up the complexion. It also improves blood circulation.

*Carrots* – Nourish and stimulate almost every system in the body. Help kidney function, reduce the risk of cancer, balance the endocrine and adrenal systems and depress blood cholesterol. Carrots are beneficial for the eyes and vision. They kill parasites and unhealthy intestinal bacteria and increase bulk elimination from the colon.

*Cauliflower* – If eaten raw, cauliflower aids bleeding gums and helps to purify the blood. It is helpful in improving the conditions of asthma, kidney and bladder disorders, high blood pressure, and constipation. Cauliflower should not be combined with other high sulfur content food.

*Celery* – Tones the vascular system, lowers blood pressure and may be useful in case of migraines. Stops the digestive fermentation of foods, purifies the bloodstream, aids digestion and helps clear up skin problems. Celery dislodges calcium deposits from joints and holds them in solution until they can be eliminated through the kidneys. Helps repair damaged ligaments and bones.

*Collards* – These dark green leafy vegetables have anti-cancer antioxidants properties. They mildly stimulate the liver and other tissues out of stagnancy.

*Corn* – Corn on the cob is high in fiber. Yellow corn is helpful in building bone and muscle and is an excellent food for the brain and nervous system. It is the easiest of all grains to digest.

*Cucumber* – Helps dissolve uric acid accumulations such as kidney and bladder stones. It destroys worms, especially tapeworms. Good for both high and low blood pressure.

Leeks – Have been prescribed for infertile women and were used internally and externally for a variety of conditions including obesity, kidney complaints, intestinal disorders and coughs.

*Lettuce* – Has large organic water content. Helps renew joints, bones, arteries and all connective tissue. Helps cure insomnia and nightmares.

*Mushrooms* – They help lower the risk of cancer, thin the blood – lowering cholesterol and aid in preventing strokes and heart attacks. Mushrooms stimulate the immune system, increase oxygen efficiency, counteract the effects of pollutants and increase resistance to disease.

*Onions* – During the Bible days, onions were used to treat colds and similar conditions. They block the viruses that cause colds and stimulate the body to produce more fluids, which in turn loosen mucus and make it easier to cough up. There are 150 chemicals in onions, and the sulfur in onion works well in stopping cancer cells. Onions block sudden increases in blood sugar and help to control diabetes. They are effective against several dangerous bacteria including the E.coli and salmonella. Onions kill bacteria responsible for illnesses ranging from diarrhea to tuberculosis.

*Peppers* – Peppers and chilies boost the secretion of saliva and stomach acids, increase peristaltic movement and feed the cell structure of the arteries, veins, and capillaries. Make body tissues more resistant to colds; promote growth and the feeling of well-being. Aid in food absorption and normalize the brain and nervous system. Chili peppers are excellent for clearing sinuses.

*Potato* – Contains a sugary carbohydrate which is readily digested and enters the bloodstream slowly to provide the constant energy we need; excellent fuel food. Potatoes are useful to those who use too much salt and high sodium foods in their diets.

*Spinach* – Helps build healthy blood; valuable for the eyes. Provides organic mineral salts required for repair and maintenance of the colon.
the digestive tract and soothes intestinal inflammation. Spinach serves as a laxative.
*Sweet Potato* – Easily digestible and good for the elimination system, ulcers, inflamed colon and those with poor circulation. Sweet Potato can bind heavy metals by sticking to the objects and pulling them out. They are very nutritious.
*Tomato* – A natural antiseptic. Tomatoes are effective in reducing liver inflammation due to hepatitis and cirrhosis.
Now, the benefits of legumes.

LEGUMES (or Bean)

Beans are in the legume family and are high in protein. They are packed with fiber to keep you regular and to keep your cholesterol and blood sugar down. You can reduce the amount of gas they produce by changing the water while they boil. Also, you may use "Beano" by adding a few drops after cooking to make your beans wind-free. Beans have a number of healthy benefits:
Flush out cholesterol – Fiber works as a bouncer for cholesterol particles. The particles get shown to the door before they can do any damage.
Increase blood flow – The protein L-arginine is in beans. It can increase blood flow. Add a few servings and see if you notice a difference.

Cut your cancer risk – What you eat could be a life or death decision. Chemical substances in beans called lignums and phytochemicals are natural cancer fighters.

*Olive (oil)* The use of high levels of olive oil offers substantially reduced risks against heart attacks and strokes. It is rich in monounsaturated fats which may lower blood cholesterol. Four to five tablespoons of olive oil daily dramatically improve the blood profiles of heart attack patients. Two-thirds of a tablespoon daily lowered blood pressure in men.

Olive oil also blocks the growth of cancer cells. Olive oil is rich in vitamin E, one of the best antioxidants available. Experts believe that those antioxidants help human cells fight off cancer. In doing so, they fortify the cells and slow down deterioration that accompanies the aging process, since the cells are healthier and live longer.

## Other uses for Olive Oil

| | |
|---|---|
| Hair | Mix with egg yolk and lemon juice; rub on hair; rinse after 5 minutes. |
| Dandruff | Mix with cologne; rub into scalp and hair; rinse after 5 minutes. |
| Dry Skin | Mix with avocado; mask the face; rinse after 10 minutes. |
| Wrinkles | Mix with lemon juice; rub into the skin at bedtime. |
| Soft Skin | Mix with salt; massage well; rinse with cool water. |
| Strong Nails | Soak nails in warm oil for 5 minutes; pat nails with white iodine. |
| Feet | Massage for rejuvenation |
| Muscles | Mix with rosemary; massage into muscles where achy. |
| Complexion | Mix equal parts with lavender oil; massage face. |
| Lowers Blood Pressure | 24 olive leaves; 8oz water; Boil 15 minutes; Cool; Drink morning and night.**(has slight laxative effect) |

| Recipe for Stir Fry Cabbage |
|---|
| |
| Ingredients: |
| |
| 1 Green cabbage - medium |
| Bell peppers – 1yellow; 1red |
| Carrots/shred-sliced – 2 cups |
| 1 Yellow onion – large |
| 1 Garlic clove – small |
| Cut of chili pepper – small (optional) |
| Olive oil – 1 tablespoon |
| Lemon pepper – dash |
| Sea Salt - dash (optional) |

Needed: 1Large Deep Frying Skillet with lid; Large Wooden Spatula; Sautee to Frying at high Temperatures

Directions:
Prepare vegetables by cleaning and washing. Next, slice bell peppers, onions, carrots, and cabbage to desired size. Mince chili pepper and garlic.

Prepare a large skillet by completely and liberally covering the bottom of the skillet with olive oil to prevent the vegetables from sticking.

With stovetop on high, place the skillet over heat; slowly add one vegetable at a time (bell peppers, onion, carrots, cabbage, garlic, chili pepper) – using a large wooden spatula to stir and turn as vegetables sautee.
Cover the skillet with a lid and reduce heat. Steam for seven minutes; Drain (if desired). Season to taste!

www.harrietwestgordon.com

*Cabbage Kills Harmful Bacteria

**WHY EXERCISE?**

There are four basic ingredients that are necessary in order for the body to sustain physical life. They are:
Oxygen (air)
Water
Food
Exercise

Food is the least important of these basic needs, as you can usually live past 40 days without food. Without water you cannot live more than four days. Without air you cannot live more than four minutes. However, without motion the body cells will slowly die!

The body needs physical activity because the tissue cells, of which the body is composed require daily stimulation to maintain their elasticity and pliability. They will become weak, sickly and begin to malfunction if they are not exercised on a regular basis. Cells will cease to function if they continue to go without exercise.

A person who exercises vigorously on a regular basis will experience fewer health problems than the person who does not exercise. Additionally, the person who exercises removes the toxins and debris from the system. Without daily exercise, tissue cells lose their elasticity. If the body does not receive a sufficient supply of oxygen, people become forgetful and eventually senile.

To live victoriously, take care of you.

**PEEL** LAUGH LEAD LEARN and LIVE LOVINGLY

"Daily movement is vital to our existence."

# CHAPTER 5
# **LOVE**
## The Ultimate Expression

"Counting the ways to love."

*In* reaching a higher level of loving yourself, it prepares you to love others, effectively. True love gives you the tenacity to PEEL off the mask of pretense, and it clears a path to transparency. During this process, you are equipped to get to the core of who *you* really are, before you are ready to experience successful relationships with others. Transforming to this healthier level has stages which must be considered:

*Human Commonalities* – coincidences of occurrences in life; with similar traits or qualities because of existence.

*Behavior Patterns* – actions which follow a schedule, habit, trend, or tradition.

*Personal Choices* – simply comfort level or preference; not to be confused with rules, laws or doctrines.

*Internalized Values* – learned or mimicked traits; unconsciously placing more worth on one's own nature or behavior.

*Core Beliefs* - foundation of trust or confidence in someone or something.

The "healthier you" transformation process brings this realization to surface: We do not speak the same Love Language.

## LOVE IS MORE THAN EMOTIONS

What is love? Love may be defined as a warm liking or affection for a person; affectionate devotion; sexual affection or passion; the relationship between sweethearts. My favorite definition of love is – God's benevolence toward mankind; strong liking for a thing. Love has a language all its own. Whether it involves, things, pets, or mates, it is important to know the Love Languages. Following is a discussion of Gary Chapman's best seller:

The Five Love Languages

Gary Chapman's book outlines five ways to express and experience what Chapman calls "love languages": 1. *gift giving*, 2. *quality time*, 3. *words of affirmation*, 4. *acts of service* (devotion), and 5. *physical touch*. According to his theory, each person has one primary and one secondary love language. My Love Languages are *Physical Touch* and *Quality Time*, while my husband's are *Gift Giving* and *Words of Affirmation*. To see my husband's beaming smile, give him a gift or stroke him with compliments. Do you know your Love Language? Do you know your significant other's Love Language? How can you find out? This is what Gary Chapman has to say.

Chapman suggests that to discover another person's love language, one must observe the way that person expresses love to others, and pay close attention to what they complain about most often, and what they request from others most often. He theorizes that people tend to naturally give love in the way that they prefer to receive love. Better communication may be accomplished when one demonstrates caring to the other person in the love language the recipient understands.

An example would be if a mate's love language is *acts of service,* he may be confused when he does the laundry for his wife and she doesn't perceive that as an act of love. She views it as simply performing household duties, because the love language she comprehends is *words of affirmation* (verbal affirmation that he loves her). She may try to use what she values, *words of affirmation*, to express her love to him, which he would not value as much as she does.

When she understands his love language and mows the lawn for him, he perceives it in his love language as an act of expressing her love for him. Likewise, if he tells her he loves her, she values that as an act of love. Often, we confuse, "soft love" or enabling, with real love. We must learn to give "tough love" through empowerment.

**STOP ENABLING AND START EMPOWERING**

Enabling may be defined as any action that allows and encourages irresponsibility and / or any act which prevents one from learning to function in the real world.

Examples of enabling are:
*Providing protection from consequences of choices.*
*Taking over responsibilities.*
*Keeping secrets instead of working as a team.*
*Accepting excuses instead of enforcing consequences.*
*Giving in to avoid hassles or complaints.*

Empowering may be defined as any action that encourages responsibility for choices, provides sound information about the world in which they live, and create opportunities for practicing life skills that will help with safety and security.

Examples of Empowerment are:
*Giving clear consistent messages about expectations, and why accountability is important.*
*Allowing others to learn from their mistakes, and experience the consequences of their choices.*

*Encouraging others to make contributions to the family. Working as a team to set boundaries and limits; then enforce consequences.*

*Empowering* versus *Enabling* will not always be an easy task; especially, when consequences are involved. Here are 10 tips to remember during the process:

## COMMUNICATING WHEN YOU ARE NOT "FEELING THE LOVE"

1. Keep your cool. Beware of losing your temper. When needed, back off.
2. Remember, when feelings are intense, thinking and judgement are impaired. Recognize that effective thinking cannot take place when emotions are high.
3. Walk through the thinking process. Say the words that you would want the other person to say, if they were able to think.
4. Be authoritative but not authoritarian. Be firm and respectful. Let them know that you will not allow them to control you. **Hint**: Heavy-handed forcefulness will backfire and increase-rather than discourage rebellion or disrespect.
5. Create future. Let them know you are a part of their support team. Be careful not to predict negativity, but let them know that the current behavior impacts their future. By creating future,

you help them to see how good decisions created good results.

6. Let them know where they stand. Have clear boundaries / 3 part success. Let them know, "These are the choices, these are the consequences, and these are the rewards."
7. Affirm their ability to make good choices. Remember, they may not love themselves; so you must let them know that you want to see them successful.
8. Be calm and consistent. Create safety by creating predictability. Consistency is imperative.
9. Distinguish between the person and the behavior. Let them know you love them but you will not tolerate the poor or negative choices and behavior.
10. Affirm their strengths. This is viable. Recognize the strengths in the behavior. Help them to see the good in their choices. Affirm the leadership and positive characteristics. Say, "I'm looking for ways which I may assist you in leading in a more effective way."

The concept of love can get confusing because people use "love" to describe different relationships. People love cars, dogs, and different things. However, the Bible is not confused about love. The Greek language uses four distinct words for love. They are:

*Agape* – supreme love. Making a deliberate choice to do good for another. A commitment based on the willful choice of the lover; not the qualities of the person receiving the love.

*Eros* – a relationship which includes physical desire, craving, and longing.

*Philos* – demonstrating care and concern friends have for each other. (Saint John 21: 15-17)

*Stergos* – affection between family members. This love should be mutual.

John is known as the Apostle of Love, and 1John offers: "Dear youth, let's not merely say that we love each other, let us show the truth by our actions. Our actions will show that we belong to the truth." 3: 18, 19. How do we know that we are born of God? We love Him and keep His commandment. Scripture further defines love for us. God's love is . . .

**Lasting** – Psalms 136
**Sacrificial** – John 15: 12,13
**Healing** – Matthew 5: 38-48
**Mutual** – Matthew 11: 27-30
**Fearless** – Romans 1: 16
**Discerning** – 1John 2: 15-17
**Generous** – Luke 10: 25-37
**Accepting** – Luke 5: 11-32
**Effective** - Because it involves not just emotions or words; but benefits to God and mankind. 1John 3: 18,19

The best summary of true love is 1Corinthians 13. Likewise, the ultimate expression of God's love is Christ who offered Himself up for the sins of the world. (John 3:16). God wants us to be intimate with Him. Just pour your heart into Him. The closer your intimacy with God, the freer your prayers will become. You will find that you do not have to hold back or (hold-up) with God. He will teach us how to begin that intimate relationship with Him. Only then are we able to give Godly love to others.

This Godly love – this *Agape* love supersedes any other love. We need to cultivate (nurture with the intent of producing a healthy product) this Christlike love and make it real in our lives. God wants to deliver this Agape love to families, workplaces, and communities through His people. Persistently look around you to find out who is in need of this kind of intentional touch of compassion and grace.

# CHAPTER 6
# **CONCLUSION**
## The PEEL ABC's

An underlying contributor to several health issues is stress. Often, people begin abnormal habits to deal with stress; such as, excessive amounts of Social Media, alcohol, drugs, unhealthy eating, elicit sex, tobacco, etc. Rather than turning to a destructive behavior pattern, try this:

**P.** **Personal** Conflict: Settle differences privately and respectfully. Try seeing the conflict from the other person's POV (Point of View) while remaining calm. Most importantly, forgive. Forgiveness is more for your journey to emotional wellness. LET IT GO!

**E.** **Events**: Avoid focusing on tragedy or unfortunate events which have occurred in your life. Stop focusing on what you do not have; instead, focus on positive events and what you do have. There will be adversities, but choose to focus on events which will bring smiles to your face.

**E.** **Everyday** Routines: Set realistic goals. Devise a functional schedule to simplify your everyday life. Increase family time and decrease expenses. Be sure to include in your schedule "Break Time" and "Play Time". You have earned it.

**Hint**: *Never allow someone else's lack of planning to create an emergency for you.*

**L.** **Lack** of Attention: Create a Support System. Do not be afraid to reach out and ask for assistance. Confide in a close friend, family member, counselor, or pastor. First and far most – pray. Through prayer, God will give you peace. Learning to *PEEL* to the core of life's stressors is a milestone on the journey to a healthy lifestyle.

Stress is also an issue for healthy cognitive development. According to a study by the National Academy of Sciences' Institute of Medicine, Cognitive decline is not inevitable. A study of what helps and what hurts cognitive functioning was included in the study. Highlights of this study follow:

### WHAT HELPS
*Exercise* – Aerobic exercise is especially beneficial for brain health, and even better when combined with strength training. Exercising for at least thirty minutes or more at a time appears to be better for brain health than shorter sessions.

*Remaining socially and intellectually active* – Activities that challenge your brain – including reading books, writing letters, and learning a new language – all help preserve brain function. So do social activities such as volunteering, playing cards, attending worship services, and talking to friends.

*Eating a balanced diet* – Although no specific diet has been proven to maintain or improve brain health, studies of the Mediterranean and DASH (Dietary Approaches to Stop Hypertension) diets justify eating less meat and consuming
more nuts, beans, whole grains, vegetables and olive oil. Fatty Acids, as in Salmon, have been shown to help cognition in some studies, though not in others.

*Getting good sleep* – Poor sleep patterns and quality are linked to cognitive impairment and Alzheimer's. Breathing disorders, such as sleep apnea, also put older people at higher risk for memory problems and dementia.

*Keeping your heart healthy* – What's good for your heart is also good for your brain. High blood pressure, high cholesterol and diabetes – especially in midlife – are linked to poor brain health
later in life. Lowering blood pressure with medication seems to help prevent brain problems.

## WHAT HURTS

*Depression* – In midlife, depression doubles the risk for cognitive decline and dementia, possibly because depression causes changes in the hippocampus. Late-life depression is also linked to dementia; especially vascular dementia, although it's unclear whether the depression may be an early symptom of undiagnosed brain health problems.

*Hearing and vision loss* – Problems hearing and seeing are both linked to trouble with thinking, memory and

socialization, and should be corrected, when possible. Older adults with hearing problems appear to have a greater rate of brain shrinkage as they age.

*Certain medications* – Anticholinergic drugs have been shown to increase the risk of dementia – these include antihistamines (Benadryl, sleep meds, antidepressants). Watch out and be aware of side effects.

*Stress* – Not only can daily stress cause memory problems, but long-term stress is connected with faster rates of decline in brain health, too. Methods to reduce stress (meditation and prayer) may help.

*Air pollution* – It may be that pollution increases heart disease, stroke and lung problems, which in turn cause problems with brain health. Or that small particles in the pollution directly harm the brain. One new study found that long-term exposure to air pollution is linked with brain shrinkage, brain damage and impaired function.

Without exercise the muscles begin to decrease in size or waste away. You can feel this when you try to use muscles that have not been exercised for a while. Above all, the most important muscle is the heart muscle. When the heart is not exercised, it starts to function improperly, arteries clog, strokes and heart attacks may result. When people suddenly exert an unexercised heart, death can occur. Mowing the lawn with force and shoveling snow are two examples that may cause sudden exertion.


**Emotional Health**

Physical health is extremely important but it is very important that we do not neglect our emotional health. It has been proven that exercise aids in the prevention of depression. Emotional problems are sicknesses that many deny. When they are recognized, it is often the symptom rather than the cause that is addressed. How many people do you know who are really happy and vibrant? The Lord wants us to be happy: John 10:10 "I am come that they might have life, and that they might have it more abundantly."

*Feelings stimulated by the mental or physical parts of our body are our emotions.* If we were to keep track of one another's emotions and placed them in two columns, one column would outweigh the other. Our emotions deeply affect our lives and the lives of those around us. All emotions are positive or negative.

**Positive Emotions** – Which happens first, the positive emotion producing a healthy body, or a healthy body producing a healthy positive mind? A healthy body has a positive effect on our whole being. When we feel joy, love, happiness, peace or contentment there is a surge of pleasure throughout the body and it emanates to those around us.

**Negative Emotions** – Negative emotions take energy from the body and hinder the body from cleansing and healing itself. Stress produces more negative emotions when the body is not able to cleanse itself. A person experiences negative emotions when his or her body does not function properly; whether it is due to lack of exercise, a headache, cold, etc. Some emotions send strong waves throughout the body. Additionally, the emotions of fear, worry, sorrow, hate, jealously or anger send negative vibes to others.

Man was created to be physically active. Yet, many people still ask, "Why do I need to exercise?" We exercise because it was one of God's commands:

"And the LORD God took the man, and put him into the garden of Eden to dress it and to keep it". Genesis 2:15

We exercise because the body cannot function properly without it. The final and one of the most important reasons is to set a good example. Now that you have learned to lead others to live with laughter and love, begin with the obvious "PEEL ABC's" in life as you manage yourself well:

Pray
Exercise
Erase names on answering devices
Limit alcohol
Avoid tobacco
Begin tasks and appointments on time
Communicate effectively
Drive safely
Expedite commitments
Fasten your seatbelts

On this journey to "Laugh Lead Learn and Live Lovingly", if there are times when it appears that 24 hours in a day just are not sufficient, remember this:

**The Mayonnaise Jar and Coffee**

A professor stood before his Philosophy class and had some items in front of him. When the class began, wordlessly, he picked up a very large and empty mayonnaise jar and proceeded to fill it with golf balls. He then asked the students if the jar was full. They agreed that it was full. The professor picked up a box of pebbles and poured them into the jar. He shook the jar lightly.

The pebbles rolled into the open areas between the golf balls. He asked the students again if the jar was full. The agreed that the jar was full, again.

The professor picked up a box of sand and poured it into the jar. The sand filled up everything else. He asked once more if the jar was full. The students responded unanimously, "Yes." The professor produced two cups of coffee from under his table and poured the entire contents into the jar; effectively filling the empty space between the sand. The students laughed. "Now" said the professor, as the laughter subsided, "I want you to recognize that this jar represents your life."

"The golf balls are the important things – God, family, youth, health, friends, favorite passions; things that if everything else was lost and only they remained, your life would be full. The pebbles are the other things that matter; as your job, house, and car. The sand is everything else; the small stuff. If you put the sand into the jar first, there is no room for the pebbles or the golf balls. The same goes for life. If you spend all of your time and energy on the small stuff, you will never have room for the things that are important to you. Pay attention to the things which are critical to your happiness. Play with your youth. Take time to get medical checkups. Take your loved ones out to dinner. Play golf more. There will always time (or businesses) to clean the house and fix the disposal. Take care of the golf balls, first; the things that really matter. Set your priorities. All the rest is just sand."

One student raised his hand and inquired, "What does the coffee represent?" The professor smiled, "I'm glad you asked. It goes to show you that no matter how full your life appears, there's always room for a cup of coffee with a friend."

## LAUGH YOUR WAY TO EXCELLENT HEALTH

**LEARN THE KINGDOM.** Learn that the Kingdom of God is within you. This is to say that all of God's values of strength, peace, health, and happiness – to mention only a few – are built in you. To stimulate good health, allow them to operate freely.

**LISTEN.** Listen to your inner thoughts. Pure joy, practiced only ten minutes each day, gets the blood circulating and clears the cobwebs from the mind. The way to be healthy is to feel and think joy.

# REFERENCES

The Holy Bible: King James and New International Versions

Gordon, Harriet West, PEEL EAT EFFICIENTLY, GHDI,inc, Lithonia, GA, 2015

www (world wide web), 2017
    Behavior Therapy
    Chapman, Gary, The Five Love Languages
    Gardner, Howard, Multiple Intelligences
    Nance, Terry, God's Armorbearer
    The Mayonnaise Jar and Coffee

# HARRIET WEST GORDON

Harriet, "triple-threat" in the fight against illiteracy, unhealthy relationships, and sedentary lifestyles is also a professional and gifted educator who is dedicated to a lifetime of serving. She has passionately and successfully served in ministry roles helping others for over 40 years. Harriet married her college sweetheart, Glenn, in September of 1978 and they are honored parents of two adult off springs who are also gifted servants: Glenn I. Gordon (Professional Hip Hop Artist; Writer-Producer), and Dawn G. Smith (Entrepreneur; Trainer, Choreographer-Dancer; M.Ed Educator). Harriet adores family life and nature. She is an advocate for education, fitness, youth, and the elderly.

She has received numerous awards for designing and leading transformational train-the-trainer developmental practices, and others. Harriet is an Intentional Intercessor, and advisor

www.ingramcontent.com/pod-product-compliance
Lightning Source LLC
LaVergne TN
LVHW052255070426
835507LV00035B/2938